PAVILION

# POCKET PAINTERS

# SEURAT

1859 – 1891

# *Seurat*

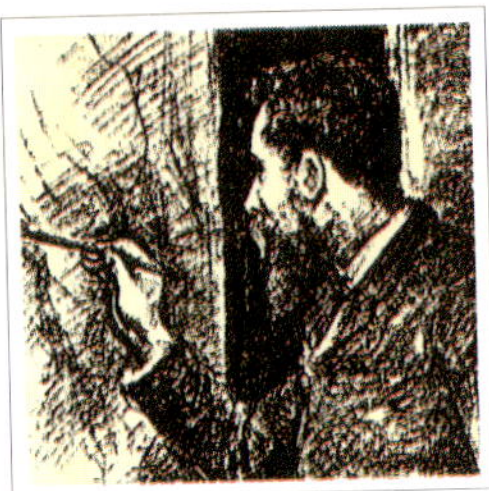

Georges Seurat (1859-1891) was at the forefront of the generation of painters which followed the Impressionists and whose work reflected the discoveries of Impressionism but marked a radical departure from it in the methods they used.

Born in Paris, Seurat entered the Ecole des Beaux-Arts in 1878, where he was trained in the classical manner by Henri Lehmann, a pupil of Ingres. Other powerful and starkly contrasting influences were the romanticism of Delacroix and the huge canvases and murals of Puvis de Chavannes, as well as theoretical writings on aesthetics and optical phenomena. Soon Seurat was working on his own theories of colour and vision, which would lead to the technique known as divisionism, or pointillism. This consists of dividing colours into pure pigments and juxtaposing tiny dots of pure colour which, if seen from the correct distance, are blended into secondary tones by the eye of the viewer.

The desire to capture the sensations received from the subtle effects of light was an obsession inherited from the Impressionists, whose fourth exhibition in 1879 made a strong impact on Seurat. However, whereas they tried to achieve it on the spot, with rapid brush-strokes fluently applied to a small canvas, he chose a much more formal, disciplined, almost scientific approach, of which divisionism was only a part. His compositions were planned in minute detail, with all their elements carefully managed, and details would be rehearsed in numerous preparatory studies before being transferred on to the canvas in his studio in the traditional manner. The result, particularly in Seurat's large-scale depictions of Parisians at leisure in the open air, is a curiously static, trance-like atmosphere which could hardly be further removed from the spontaneity of Impressionism.

By 1886 Seurat was the acknowledged leader of the group of painters, including Paul Signac, who were known as the neo-Impressionists.

Even Impressionists were drawn into it, notably Camille Pissarro, who experimented at length with divisionism in the late 1880s before rejecting it as too laborious and cerebral for his purposes. It was left to other members of the group to pursue the discoveries made by Seurat, for he died suddenly of diptheria at the age of 31. Others, indeed, have claimed some of the credit for them, but it was undoubtedly the intellectual Seurat who formulated the basic theories of divisionism, and although he was prevented from developing them, it can fairly be said that in a career lasting little more than ten years he had accomplished the remarkable feat of creating an entirely new and self-contained system of painting. ◪

*The Gleaner*

Conté crayon

1881 – 2

31.4 × 23.7 cm

The opposition of light and dark in the drawings which Seurat produced in his early twenties suggest that he may, like van Gogh, have been influenced by Millet. He would continue to use conté crayon in his preparatory sketches for major paintings such as *The Bathers*.

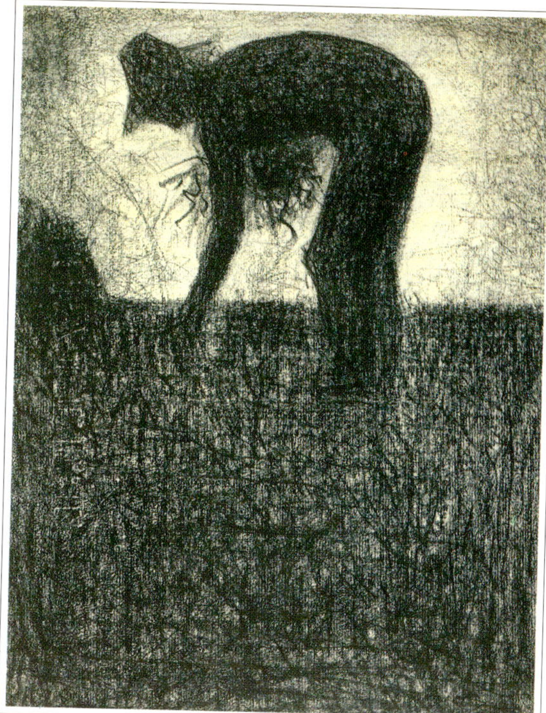

***The Stone-breaker***

Oil on panel

1882

16.2 × 25.5 cm

In the paintings of agricultural labourers which Seurat produced in the period following the fourth Impressionist exhibition, he gave his figures strong physical presence and sometimes, as here, showed them in vigorous activity. Figures were to have a much less animated role in his later, divisionist work.

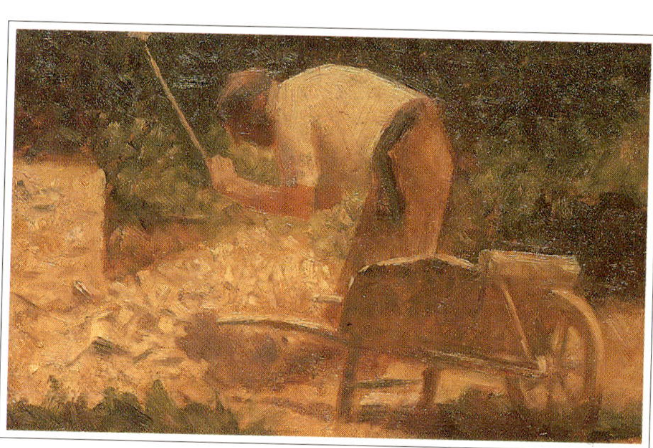

***A Field in Summer***

Oil on canvas
1883
16 × 25 cm

Seurat found subjects for many of his early landscape paintings in the countryside around Le Raincy, to the east of Paris, where his reclusive father had a second home and spent most of his time, while the family lived in the city.

*Sunset*

Oil on canvas

1881 – 2

15.7 × 25 cm

Of the Impressionists whose work Seurat saw in the 1870s, it was Pissarro who provided most encouragement. He became not only a close friend of Seurat but also, for a time, a follower. His recruitment of Seurat and Signac for the eighth Impressionist exhibition of 1886 led to Monet, Sisley and Renoir staying away.

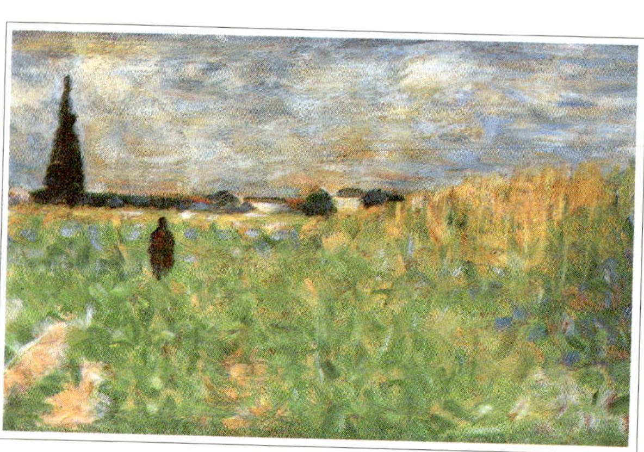

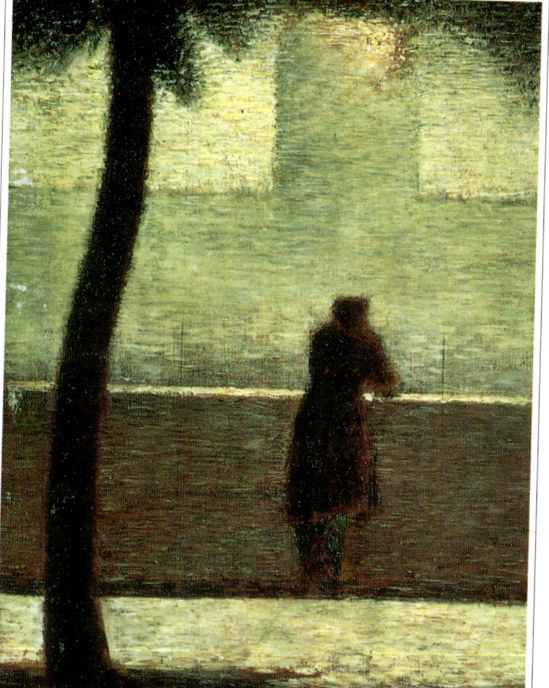

*The Watering Can*

Oil on panel
c.1883
24.8 × 15.5 cm

Seurat liked to take the kind of object which would normally appear as a detail and place it firmly in the foreground as an integral part of the design. The watering-can was painted at his father's garden at Le Raincy.

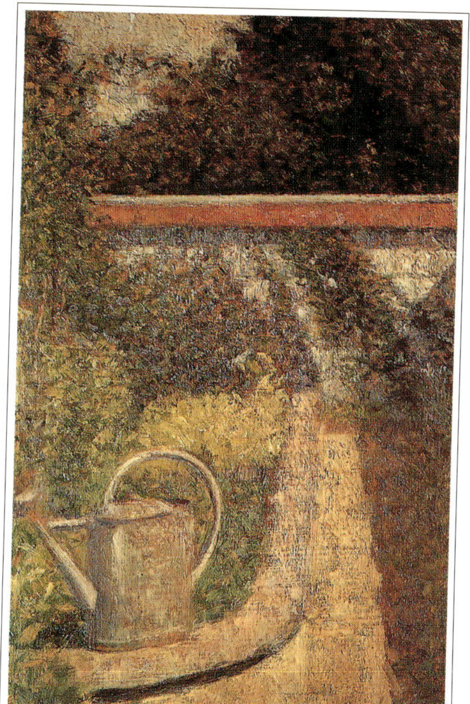

***The Bathers at Asnières***

Oil on canvas
1883 – 4
201 × 301 cm

Seurat's first great work, *The Bathers,* marks his point of departure from Impressionism. The popular bathing-place is essentially Impressionist subject matter, but the orderly placing of the elements and the monumental stillness are very much his own. He produced studies of various possible elements – including horses – before working out their spatial relationships.

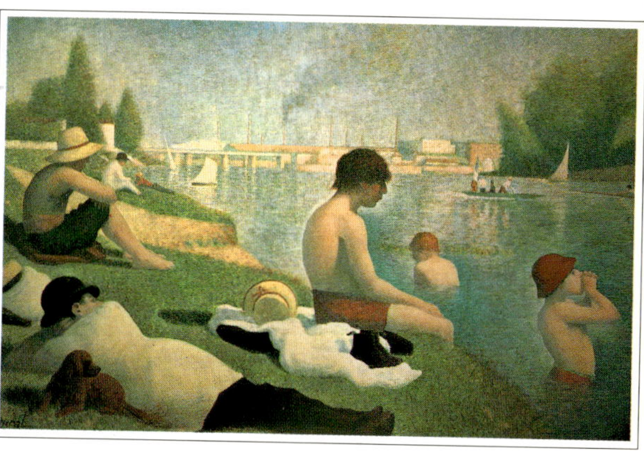

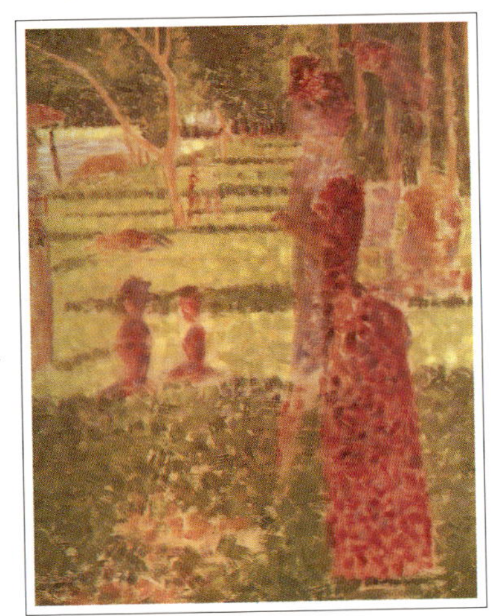

***Couple Walking***
Study for *Sunday Afternoon on the Ile de la Grande Jatte*

Oil on canvas
1884 – 5
81.5 × 65.2 cm

Left – Seurat's work on *La Grande Jatte* coincided with the formulation of his divisionist technique. As a result, although the finished painting became the first major divisionist work to be exhibited, preparatory studies such as this one still have some of the spontaneity of Impressionism.

Overleaf – The fact that some have seen in this gallery of promenading Parisians ironic social comment that Seurat himself disclaimed, is probably due to his meticulous planning and revolutionary divisionism, which combine to produce an artificial, frieze-like effect. Exhibited at the 1886 Impressionist exhibition, Seurat's masterpiece caused a sensation.

***Sunday Afternoon on the Ile de la Grande Jatte***

Oil on canvas

1884 – 6

207 × 308 cm

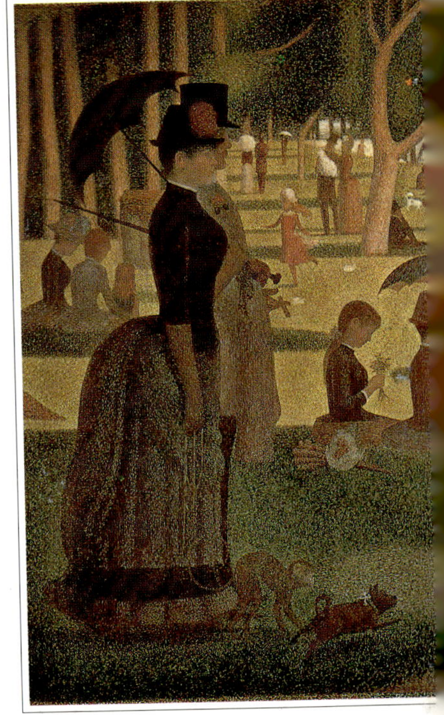

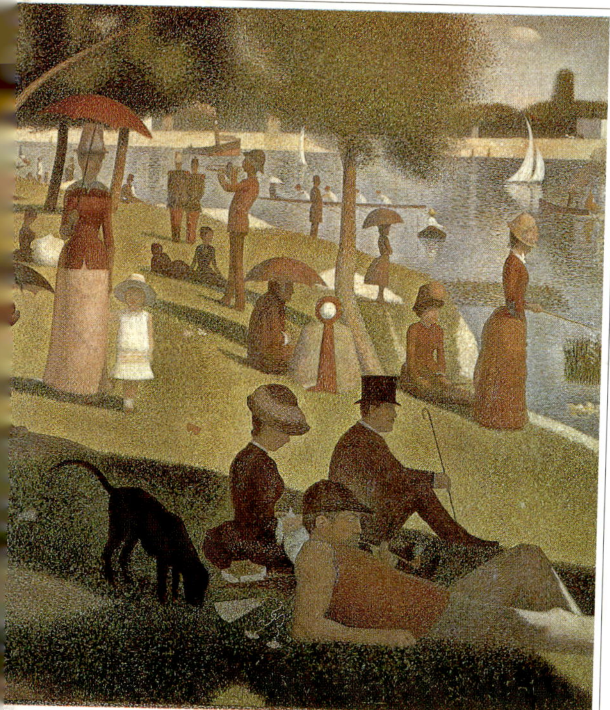

***The Seine at Courbevoie***

Oil on canvas
1885 – 6
81.5 × 65 cm

The landscapes of Seurat's divisionist maturity are perfectly controlled, if somewhat soporific arrangements. This one is enlivened only by the small dog and, to a lesser extent, its mistress, a refugee from *La Grande Jatte* who must be beginning to suspect that she is only wanted for her verticality.

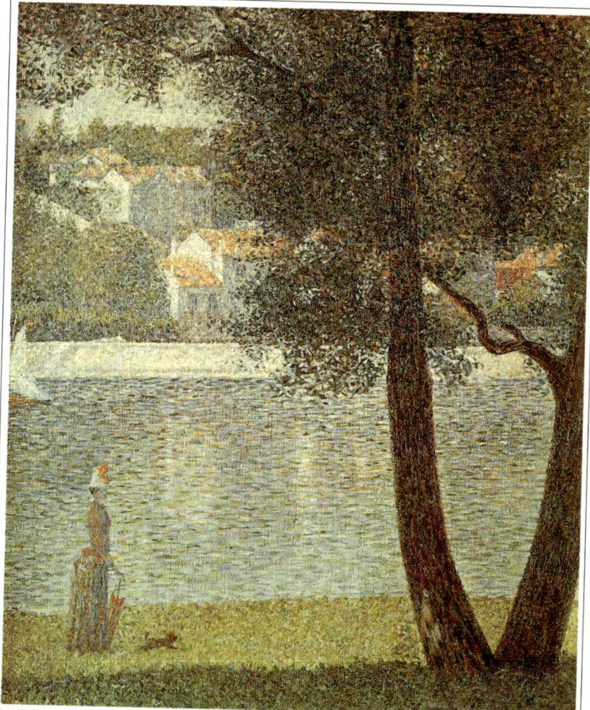

***The Beach at Bas-Butin, Honfleur***

Oil on canvas

1886

66 × 82 cm

Seurat spent the summers of 1885 and 1886 at various locations along the Normandy coastline, painting seascapes and working out more fully his theories of divisionism. He was to continue dividing his time between Paris and the Channel coast.

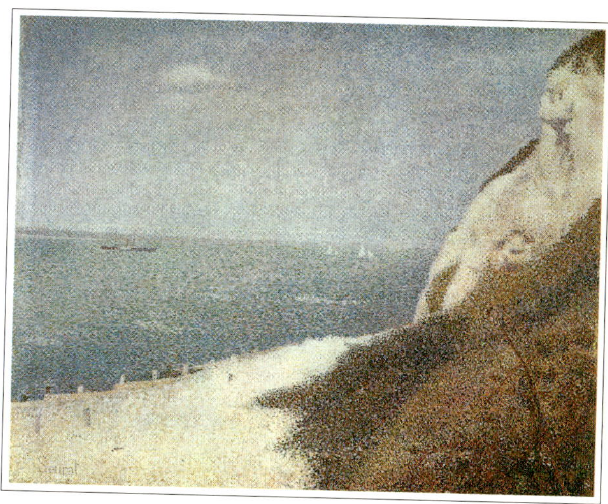
Seurat

***The 'Maria' at Honfleur***

Oil on canvas

1886

54.5 × 64.5 cm

Through his systematic control of form and colour, Seurat produced a sense of order, harmony and timelessness, thus distancing himself from the casualness and immediacy of Impressionism.

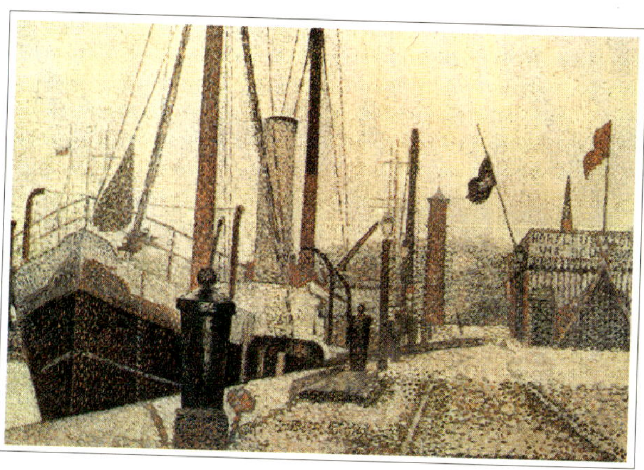

***Seated Model, Profile***
Study for
*The Models*

Oil on panel
1886 – 7
24 × 15 cm

For *The Models,* one of Seurat's largest and most ambitious compositions, the same model was posed in three different attitudes in the artist's studio. Numerous preparatory studies were carried out in both charcoal and oils.

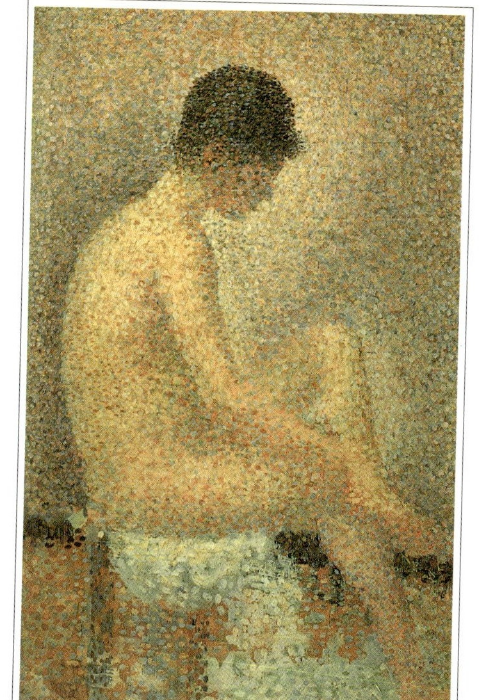

***Seated Model, Back View***
Study for *The Models*

Oil on panel
1886 – 7
24.5 × 15.5 cm

The finished painting of *The Models* is divided down the centre by a standing figure, facing the viewer impassively. This seated figure is on the left, her top half silhouetted against the canvas of *La Grande Jatte,* which occupies almost half of the background.

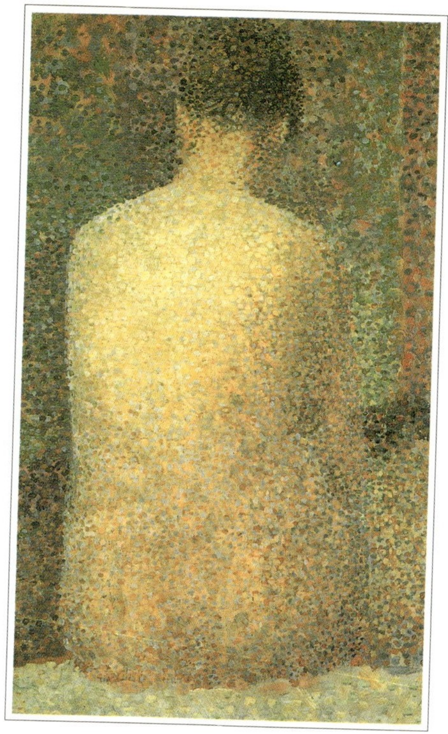

***The Bridge at Courbevoie***

Oil on canvas

1886 – 7

46 × 55 cm

The subordination of content to design makes this one of Seurat's more abstract landscapes. The familiar flat horizontals are joined by a series of precise verticals, including the perfunctory figures, thus dividing the central area into rectangular spaces.

Overleaf - In its subject matter about as far removed from *The Bridge at Courbevoie* as it could be, *La Parade* nevertheless echoes the landscape's geometrical composition with remarkable fidelity, the larger figures, like its crooked tree, providing relief within the rigidly vertical pattern.

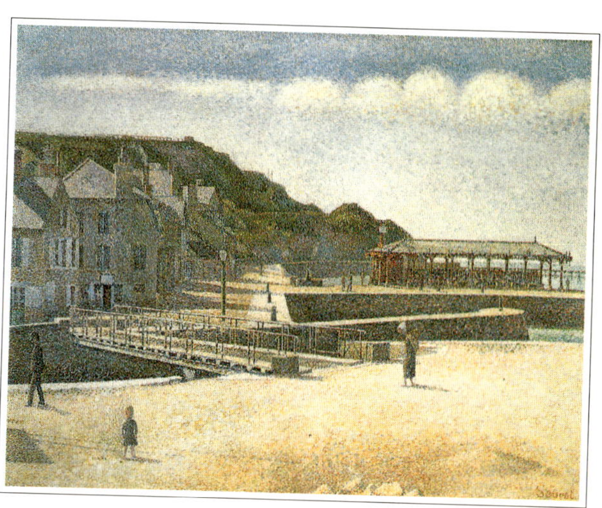

*The Eiffel Tower*

Oil on wood

1889

24.2 × 15.2 cm

Nothing can have seemed more modern in 1889 than Seurat's treatment of the Eiffel Tower. There is no pretence of rendering faithfully what was before his eye, and the structure itself was not yet even complete at the time.

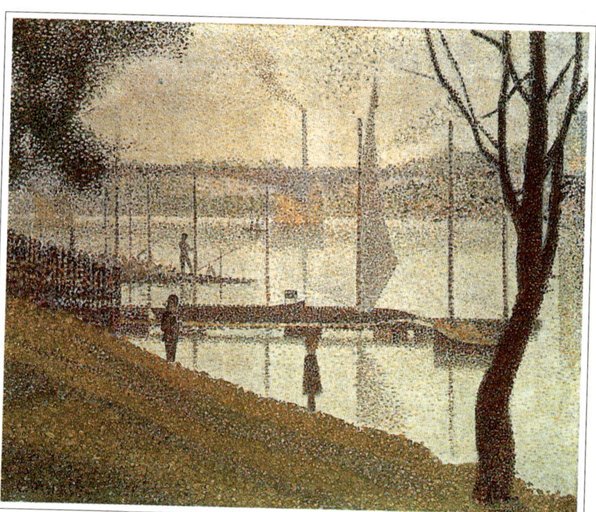

**_La Parade_**
(or: _Invitation to the Side-show)_

Oil on canvas
1887 – 8
99.5 × 150 cm

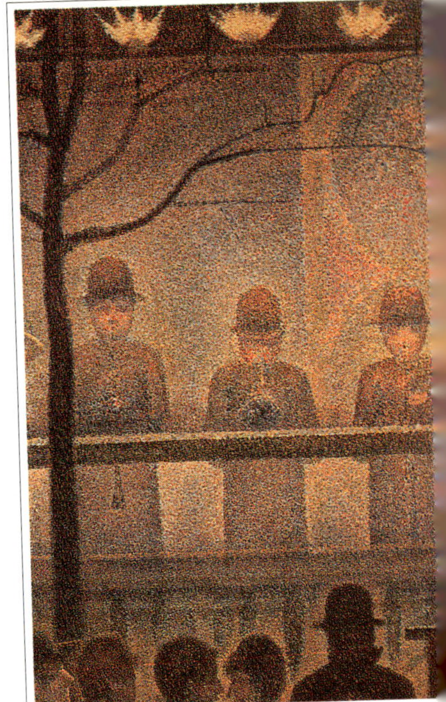

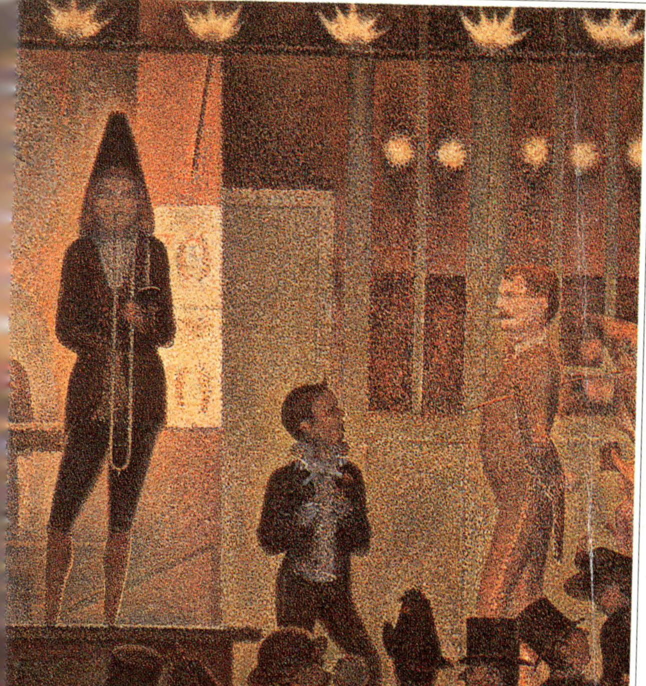

***The Harbour and Quays at Port-en-Bessin***

Oil on canvas
1888
67 × 84.3 cm

The subjects of Seurat's later work tended to be either figures in indoor settings or landscapes more or less devoid of people. This is a rare example of an outdoor scene in which the figures seem to exist in their own right rather than as mere components of the design.

Study for
***Le Chahut***

Oil on panel
1889 – 90
21.5 × 16.5 cm

Although the cabaret *milieu* beloved of Degas and Toulouse-Lautrec loses its seediness and character when filtered through Seurat's system, the study succeeds brilliantly in design terms – and the painting itself was to become an icon for the Cubists.

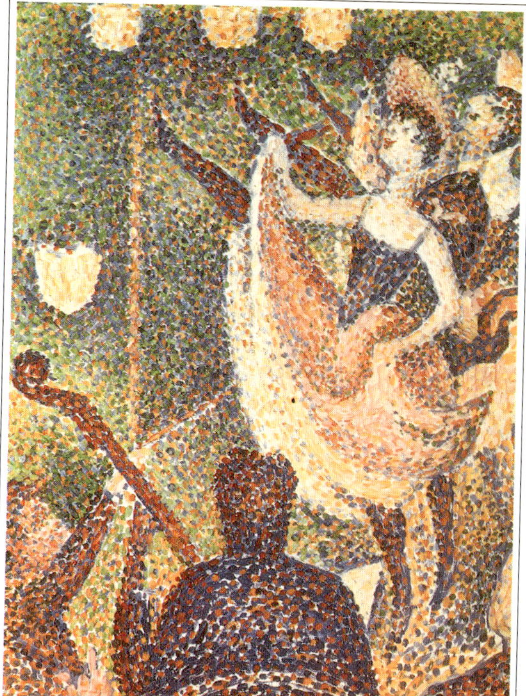

*Young Woman Powdering Herself*

Oil on canvas

1889 – 90

95 × 79 cm

Seurat was only 31 when he died, but his theories and example had already had a major influence on others, and later works such as this masterly, admiring portrait of Madeleine Knobloch, his common-law wife and the mother of his son, demonstrate the sheer distance he had travelled artistically in his brief career.

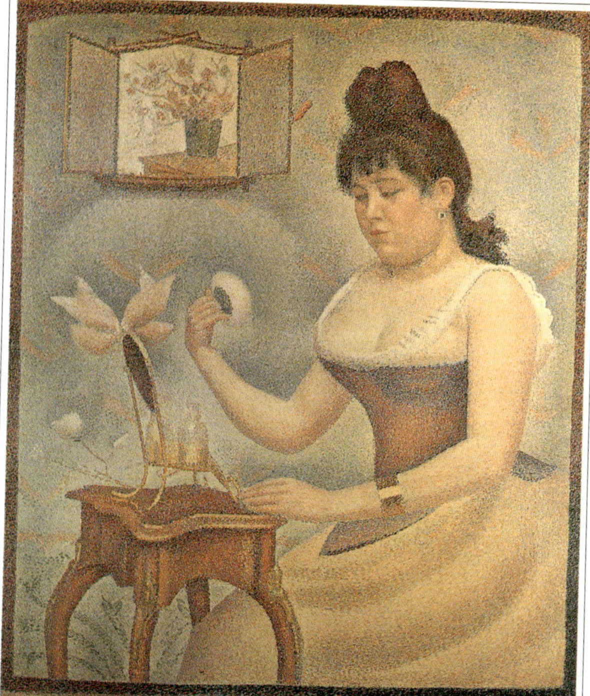

**All photographic material supplied by**
**The Bridgeman Art Library, London**
except p2 *Seurat* by Maximilien Luce:
Bibliothèque National, Paris.

Cover: *Sunday Afternoon on the Ile de la Grande Jatte* (detail):
Art Institute of Chicago;
p7 *The Gleaner:*
British Museum, London;
p9 *The Stonebreaker:*
Private Collection;
p11 *A Field in Summer:*
Christie's, London;
p13 *Sunset:*
City of Bristol Museum and Art Gallery;
p15 *Man Leaning on a Parapet:*
Private Collection;
p17 *The Watering Can;*
Private Collection;
p19 *The Bathers at Asnières:*
National Gallery, London;
p20 *Couple Walking:*
Private Collection;

p22/23 *Sunday Afternoon on the Ile de la Grande Jatte:*
Art Institute of Chicago;
p25 *The Seine at Coubevoie:*
Private Collection;
p27 *The Beach at Bas-Butin,* Honfleur:
Musée des Beaux-Arts, Tournai,
p29 *The Maria at Honfleur:*
Narodni Museum, Prague;
p31 *Seated Model,* Profile:
Palais De Tokyo, Paris;
p33 *Seated Model, Back View:*
Musée D'Orsay, Paris/Giraudon;
p35 *The Bridge at Courbevoie:*
Courtauld Institute Galleries, London;
p37 *La Parade* (detail):
Metropolitan Museum of Art, New York;
p39 *The Harbour and Quays at Port-en-Bessin:*
Minneapolis Society of Fine Arts, Minnesota;
p41 *The Eiffel Tower:*
San Francisco Museum of Art, California;
p43 *Study for Le Chahut:*
Courtauld Institute Galleries, London;
p45 *Young Woman Powdering Herself:*
Courtauld Institute Galleries, London.

First published in Great Britain in 1994 by
**Pavilion Books Limited**
26 Upper Ground, London SE1 9PD

Designed by Andrew Barron & Collis Clements Associates



A CIP catalogue record for this book is available from the British Library

ISBN 1 85793 367 2

Printed and bound in Italy.

2 4 6 8 10 9 7 5 3 1

This book may be ordered by post direct from the publisher.
Please contact the Marketing Department.
But try your bookshop first.

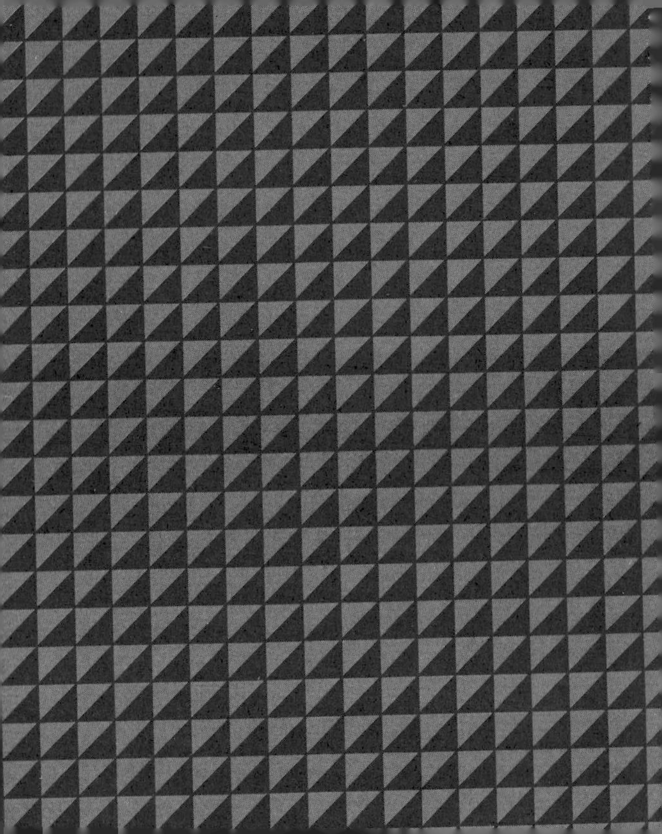